DISCOVERING
CENTRAL AMERICA

Nicaragua

DISCOVERING
CENTRAL AMERICA

Nicaragua

Charles J. Shields

Mason Crest Publishers
Philadelphia

Mason Crest Publishers
370 Reed Road
Broomall PA 19008
www.masoncrest.com

First printing

1 3 5 7 9 8 6 4 2

Library of Congress Cataloging-in-Publication Data
on file at the Library of Congress

ISBN 1-59084-097-6

DISCOVERING
CENTRAL AMERICA

Belize
Central America: Facts and Figures
Costa Rica
El Salvador

Guatemala
Honduras
Nicaragua
Panama

Discovering Central America

James D. Henderson

CENTRAL AMERICA is a beautiful part of the world, filled with generous and friendly people. It is also a region steeped in history, one of the first areas of the New World explored by Christopher Columbus. Central America is both close to the United States and strategically important to it. For nearly a century ships of the U.S. and the world have made good use of the Panama Canal. And for longer than that breakfast tables have been graced by the bananas and other tropical fruits that Central America produces in abundance.

Central America is closer to North America and other peoples of the world with each passing day. Globalized trade brings the region's products to world markets as never before. And there is promise that trade agreements will soon unite all nations of the Americas in a great common market. Meanwhile improved road and air links make it easy for visitors to reach Middle America. Central America's tropical flora and fauna are ever more accessible to foreign visitors having an interest in eco-tourism. Other visitors are drawn to the region's dazzling Pacific Ocean beaches, jewel-like scenery, and bustling towns and cities. And everywhere Central America's wonderful and varied peoples are outgoing and welcoming to foreign visitors.

These eight books are intended to provide complete, up-to-date information on the five countries historians call Central America (Guatemala, El Salvador, Honduras, Nicaragua, Costa Rica), as well as on Panama (technically part of South America) and Belize (technically part of North America). Each volume contains chapters on the land, history, economy, people, and cultures of the countries treated. And each country study is written in an engaging style, employing a vocabulary appropriate to young students.

Women make pottery in San Juan de Oriente.

All volumes contain colorful illustrations, maps, and up-to-date boxed information of a statistical character, and each is accompanied by a chronology, a glossary, a bibliography, selected Internet resources, and an index. Students and teachers alike will welcome the many suggestions for individual and class projects and reports contained in each country study, and they will want to prepare the tasty traditional dishes described in each volume's recipe section.

This eight-book series is a timely and useful addition to the literature on Central America. It is designed not just to inform, but also to engage school-aged readers with this important and fascinating part of the Americas.

Let me introduce this series as author Charles J. Shields begins each volume: *¡Hola!* You are discovering Central America!

(Opposite) Fishermen launch dugout canoes at sunset from the beach at Puerto Cabezas. (Right) Nicaragua is located in a region where earthquakes and other natural disasters are fairly common. This man's house in Laguna de Apoyo was destroyed in July 2000 by an strong earthquake that measured 5.9 on the Richter scale.

1 A Land Rich in Natural Resources

¡HOLA! ARE YOU discovering Nicaragua? It's a land of beaches lapped by sparkling seawater, deep forests, long winding rivers, colonial cities, ancient sites thousands of years old, and a huge freshwater lake—the only lake in the world with sharks in it!

Central America's Largest Country

Nicaragua is bordered on the north by Honduras, on the east by the Caribbean Sea, on the south by Costa Rica, and on the west by the Pacific Ocean. Nicaragua is the largest country of Central America, covering an area of 50,464 sq. miles (129,494 sq. km). Nicaragua's maximum length from north to south is about 275 miles (440 km), and its maximum width from

Quick Facts: The Geography of Nicaragua

Location: Middle America, bordering both the Caribbean Sea and the North Pacific Ocean, between Costa Rica and Honduras.

Geographic coordinates: 13'00"N, 85'00"W

Area: (slightly smaller than New York)
total: 129,494 sq. km
land: 120,254 sq. km
water: 9,240 sq. km

Borders: Costa Rica, 309 km; Honduras, 922 km; coastline: 910 km.

Terrain: extensive Atlantic coastal plains rising to central interior mountains; narrow Pacific coastal plain interrupted by volcanoes.

Climate: tropical in lowlands, cooler in the highlands.

Elevation extremes:
lowest point: Pacific Ocean 0 m
highest point: Mogotón 2,103 m

Natural resources: gold, silver, copper, tungsten, lead, zinc, timber, fish.

Land use:
arable land: 9 percent
permanent crops: 1 percent
permanent pastures: 46 percent
forests and woodland: 27 percent
other: 17 percent
Irrigated land: 880 sq. km

east to west is about 280 miles (450 km). In size, it is a little larger than the state of New York. Lake Nicaragua—the one with sharks in it—is in the southwest. With an area of 3,156 square miles (8,157 sq. km), it is the largest lake in Central America. The country's physical geography divides it into three major zones: Pacific lowlands; the wetter, cooler central highlands, and the Caribbean lowlands.

Pacific Lowlands: Where Most Live

The Pacific lowlands, lakes, and western volcanic mountains of Nicaragua—some of which are active—contain the majority of the country's population, most of its cities, and most of its industry.

Nicaragua is mainly urban. In other words, most people live in towns and cities on the Pacific side of Nicaragua. Managua, the capital, is the largest, most developed city in Nicaragua, with a population of nearly 1 million. There are six freshwater lakes near the city of Managua: Lake Managua; Lake Tiscapa; Lake Asososca, which acts as the city's reservoir of drinking water; Lake Jiloá, which has bitter-tasting water and is a favorite bathing resort; Lake Masaya, which is prized for its swimming and fishing facilities; and Lake Nejapa, where the sulfur-smelling waters are said to have healing properties. The urban centers of León, Granada, Masaya, and Chinandega are all in the west, too.

Because western Nicaragua is located where two major *tectonic* plates collide, earthquakes and volcanic eruptions happen frequently on the Pacific side. Although fumes and ash from volcanoes have damaged farm-land at times, earthquakes have been by far more destructive to life and property. Hundreds of shocks occur each year, some of which cause severe damage. Managua was almost destroyed in 1931 and again in 1972 by earthquakes.

Farming in the Central Highlands

The triangular area known as the central highlands lies northeast and east of the Pacific lowlands. The mountain ranges running through this region include the Cordillera Entre Ríos on the Honduras border; the Cordilleras Isabelia and Dariense in the north-central area; and the Huapí, Amerrique, and Yolaina mountains in the southeast. The mountains are highest in the north. Mogotón Peak, at 6,900 ft (2,103 m) in the Cordillera

Entre Ríos, is the highest point in the country.

Forests of oak and pine cover the Pacific-facing slopes of this rugged *terrain*. Protected from Caribbean storms by high ridges, these slopes have attracted farmers since Spanish colonial times, and are now well settled. Deep valleys drain easterly toward the Caribbean Sea. On the eastern slopes, rainforests, nourished by tropical weather from the Caribbean, make farming difficult. The rainforests on the eastern side are home to small communities of *Amerindians*.

Hot and Humid Lowlands in the East

The hot and humid eastern half of Nicaragua has low, level plains. Among the widest Caribbean lowlands in Central America, these plains average 60 miles (100 km) in width. The soil is generally salt-soaked and *infertile*. The coastline is broken up by river mouths and deltas and large coastal lagoons, as well as by the coral reefs, islands, *cays*, and banks. There are a few towns on the east Caribbean coast—Bluefields and Puerto Cabezas are the largest—but the population on that side of the country is much smaller.

Nicaragua's four principal rivers—the San Juan, Coco, Río Grande de Matagalpa, and Prinzapolka—flow downward from the central highlands, through the Caribbean Lowlands, and empty into the Caribbean Sea.

Nicaragua's Climate

Temperature varies little with the seasons in Nicaragua. The elevation of the land is what makes the difference.

The *tierra caliente*, or the "hot land," is characteristic of the foothills and lowlands from sea level to about 1,000 feet of elevation. Here, daytime temperatures average 80° to 95° F (30° to 35° C), and night temperatures drop to around 70° F (21° C) most of the year. The *tierra templada*, or the "temperate land," is characteristic of most of the central highlands, where elevations range between 1,000 and 2,000 feet (305 to 610 meters). Here, daytime temperatures are mild (70° to 75° F; 21° to 23° C), and nights are cool (50 ° F; 10° C). *Tierra fría*, the "cold land," is found only on and near the highest peaks of the central highlands, at elevations above 2,000 feet (610 meters). Daytime averages in this region are around 52° F (11° C), with nighttime lows below 45° F (7° C).

Nicaragua is often buffeted by hurricanes and tropical storms. This 89-year-old man is carrying his few possessions through the floodwaters and driving rain of Hurricane Keith in October 2000.

Rainfall, however, does vary greatly in Nicaragua. First, rainfall is seasonal—May through October is the rainy season, and December through April is the driest period. Second, the Caribbean lowlands are the wettest section of Central America, receiving between 8 and 16 feet of rain annually. The western slopes of the central highlands and the Pacific lowlands receive considerably less annual rainfall, being protected from humid Caribbean *trade winds* by the peaks of the central highlands.

During the rainy season, eastern Nicaragua often floods along the upper and middle sections of all major rivers. In addition, destructive tropical storms and hurricanes, particularly from July through October, buffet the coast. The high winds and floods accompanying these storms can cause widespread destruction. Now and then, sudden heavy rains (called *papagayo* storms) follow a cold front and sweep from the north through both eastern and western Nicaragua from November through March.

Plants and Animals in Abundance

Nicaragua is fortunate to have some of the best and most abundant resources in Central America. Its volcanic soil is ideal for growing rich crops. Nicaragua also has the largest forests of commercially valuable trees in Central America, covering one-third of the country. Nicaragua's forests contain valuable cedar, mahogany, and pine timber as well as *quebracho* (axbreaker), *guaiacum* (a type of iron-wood), *guapinol* (a tree that yields *resin*), and *medlar* (a tree that produces a crabapple-like fruit).

This peccary, a type of pig native to the Americas, grazes in one of Nicaragua's many national parks. Like all Central American countries, Nicaragua has a wide variety of animal and plant life.

There is also a fascinating variety of wildlife, such as pumas, jaguars, ocelots, margays, various monkeys, deer, and peccaries. Birds range from eagles to egrets to macaws and pelicans. Reptiles include crocodiles, snakes, turtles, and lizards; and a variety of toads, frogs, fishes, and mollusks. Unfortunately, there is a brisk business in trapping deer, pumas, monkeys, macaws, and parrots and selling them.

National Parks and Nature Preserves

Thirty-one miles south of the border with Honduras is Cerro Saslaya National Park, an area of over 37,000 acres containing some of the most diverse plant and animal life in Nicaragua. Scientific tours, river trips, observation areas, and other activities are popular among researchers and tourists alike.

The Río Indio Biological Reserve is an enormous world-biosphere reserve covering more than three-quarters of a million acres. It is located at the extreme southeast corner of the Caribbean coast, at the border with Costa Rica near the town of Bluefields. It includes rivers, a seacoast, and lowland plains. A tropical rainforest inside the reserve contains medicinal plants, orchids, deer, monkeys, tapirs, and other mammals, as well as manatees and waterfowl in the marshy areas.

The Miskitos Key National Park is a cluster of 80 coral islands located offshore and slightly to the north of Puerto Cabezas. This marine biological reserve is considered to be one of the loveliest recreational areas in Central America, and is known for its sport fishing and diving.

In December 1972 a series of earthquakes devastated Managua (opposite), the largest city in Nicaragua. (Right) U.S. President Ronald Reagan poses with Adolfo Calero and other Contra leaders in the White House in August 1987. The scandal that erupted over U.S. support of the Nicaraguan rebels dogged the last years of Reagan's administration.

2 A Troubled History

NICARAGUA'S HISTORY is a troubled one. Ruthless dictators, corruption, and repression appear as stains on its past. In addition, natural disasters plague the country. Earthquakes twice destroyed the capital city of Managua in the last century, and hurricanes are an annual threat.

Fortunately, the course of Nicaragua's history has changed somewhat for the better in recent years. In 1990, the Sandinista rebels, who had seized control of the country from a brutal dictator 11 years earlier, handed over the reins of government to the democratically elected president. Since then, the country has continued working toward democracy and human rights for all of its citizens. Nicaragua enters the 21st century hoping to overcome its past.

From Ancient Legends to Conquest

According to Amerindian legend, there are prehistoric footprints near Managua, Nicaragua, left by people fleeing to Lake Managua from a volcanic eruption almost 10,000 years ago. Much later, wanderers found that the soil created by the volcanic ash and minerals was excellent for growing food like beans and maize (corn). As a result, small permanent agricultural communities developed in Nicaragua, although civilization never became as advanced as that of the mighty Aztec and Mayan empires. Nevertheless, the Amerindians of this region were skilled in making stone carvings, pottery, and gold jewelry.

In 1502, Christopher Columbus sighted the coast of the Americas. Twenty years later, the Spanish conquistador Gil González Dávila made the first attempt to gain a foothold in what would become Nicaragua. Although he claimed to have converted some 30,000 natives to Christianity, carried off wagonloads of gold, and discovered a possible water route between the Atlantic and Pacific oceans, González was eventually run out by angry Amerindians. Their leader was a chief named Nicarao, for whom Nicaragua is now named. Just two years later, however, in 1524, Spanish colonization began in earnest under Francisco Hernández de Córdoba. Hernandez founded the settlements of Léon and Granada, and Nicaragua became an official part of the Spanish Empire. These two cities still exist today.

The Spanish conquest was disastrous for the Indians of Nicaragua's Pacific coast. Within three decades, an estimated Indian population of one million plummeted to a few tens of thousands. Half of the *indigenous* people died of Old World diseases, and thousands more were sold into slavery in other New World Spanish colonies.

However, after these crises, the Spanish empire lost interest in Nicaragua, turning its attention to further expansion elsewhere. Granada and León emerged as competing centers of power, although they both suffered from frequent attacks by Caribbean pirates. Late in the 1600s, Great Britain formed an alliance with the Miskito Indians of the Caribbean coastal region, where the trading outpost of Bluefields had been established. The British settled on the Mosquito Coast, as it came to be known, and for a time (1740–86) the region came under British rule.

In the early 19th century, Spanish power went into a rapid decline. As Napoleon's armies marched across Europe, Spain was too deeply involved in war to pay attention to Central America. Its colonies there used the opportunity to break away as independent nations.

Spain officially granted independence to Nicaragua when Guatemala declared independence for all of Central America in 1821.

New Foreign Adventures

After Spain withdrew, Nicaragua lay open to new foreign adventures. The British government strengthened its hold on Bluefields, and in 1848 seized the small Caribbean port of San Juan del Norte, renaming it Greytown.

The discovery of gold in California renewed attention in Nicaragua. American financier Cornelius Vanderbilt began a steamship and carriage operation between Greytown on the Caribbean coast and the Pacific Ocean, making Nicaragua a point of passage between the two oceans long before there was a Panama Canal.

The contest between the powerful towns of Léon and Granada continued, however. In 1855, American adventurer William Walker took advantage of the rivalry to capture and loot Granada at the head of a renegade army. He declared himself president and sought statehood from the United States. However, Vanderbilt's transit company supported the Nicaraguans in driving Walker out of the country in 1856, foiling his plans to take over all of Central America, one country at a time.

In 1893, Jose Santos Zelaya led an anti-foreigner revolt that gained him the presidency of Nicaragua and removed the Bluefields region from British control. The United States, predicting that Zelaya would *destabilize* Central America, intervened with U.S. troops to protect American lives and property. With the exception of a brief period in 1925–26, the United States maintained troops in Nicaragua from 1912 until 1933. Beginning in 1927, U.S. marines fought a running battle with rebel forces led by General Augusto Sandino, who wanted the United States out of Nicaragua. The United States finally withdrew its troops in 1933.

The Somoza Dynasty

The departure of U.S. troops signaled the start of a new round of disorder. National Guard Commander Anastasio Somoza Garcia outmaneuvered his political opponents, including Sandino, who was *assassinated* by National Guard officers, and took over the presidency in 1936. Somoza ruled harshly until his own assassination in 1956. He was succeeded by his son Luis, who shared the presidency with trusted family friends until his death in 1967. Another son, Major General Anastasio Somoza Debayle, became president that year. He continued the Somoza tradition of ruling Nicaragua with an iron fist through the National Guard, relying on the United States for political support, pursuing his political enemies, and amassing an enormous family fortune.

On December 23, 1972, an earthquake leveled the city of Managua, leaving 6,000 dead and 20,000 injured. Somoza declared *martial* law, as if a state of war existed. International aid sent to rebuild Managua found its way into the dictator's hands instead, fueling the anger of his opponents.

> ## Did You Know?
> - The national tree of Nicaragua is the *madroño*, which becomes covered in white flowers during the summer. This tree was chosen because of the elegance of its shape and its usefulness.
> - The national flower is the *sacuanjoche*, also called the May Flower because that is its flowering month.
> - The national bird of Nicaragua is the *guardabarranco*, which lives in the forests of Nicaragua and likes to perch on branches and wave its tail feathers back and forth like a pendulum.

A mass uprising ended the Somoza dynasty in 1979. A year earlier, an editor of the anti-Somoza newspaper *La Prensa* had been assassinated. Nicaraguans blamed Somoza. Anti-Somoza *guerrilla* forces under the leadership of the Sandinista National Liberation Front (FSLN)—*leftists* who took their name from General Augusto Sandino—escalated their guerrilla war against the government. The country erupted into civil war. The United States, expecting that a Communist *regime* would seize power, urged Somoza to resign so that a moderate group could run the country instead. After seven weeks of fighting, Somoza fled the country on July 17, 1979, and the Sandinistas assumed power on July 19.

The Sandinista Era

Although the Sandinistas promised to remain neutral in Central American politics, American president Ronald Reagan accused them of supplying arms to Communist rebels in El Salvador with the aid of Cuba and the Soviet Union. On January 23, 1981, the United States suspended its aid to Nicaragua as a result. The Reagan administration stepped up its opposition to the Sandinista government by aiding a resistance movement, the Contras, in its efforts to overthrow the Sandinistas.

Elections in Nicaragua on November 4, 1984, resulted in Daniel Ortega, the Sandinista leader, winning the presidency. The United States countered by imposing a *trade embargo* in 1985. Ortega declared a state of national emergency and suspended all *civil rights*. The war between the Sandinistas and the Contras intensified from 1985 to 1987, with members of the United States Congress accusing the Reagan

Contra guerrillas move carefully through the jungle. The war in Nicaragua lasted through most of the 1980s, ending after a peace agreement was signed in 1987.

administration of secretly supplying arms and money to the Contras without approval. The issue became known as the Iran-Contra Affair.

Negotiations sponsored by the Contadora (neutral Latin American) nations failed to end the war in Nicaragua. However, Oscar Arias Sánchez, president of Costa Rica, proposed a peace plan that succeeded. Five Central American presidents signed Sánchez's peace plan in Guatemala City in 1987, an accomplishment for which he received the Nobel Peace Prize.

By then, however, Nicaragua was an economic and social disaster zone as a result of the strife. The Sandinista government agreed to nationwide elections in February 1990. In these elections, which were proclaimed fair by international observers, Nicaraguan voters elected as their president the candidate of the National Opposition Union, Violeta Barrios de Chamorro, the widow of slain *La Prensa* newspaper editor Pedro Joaquín Chamorro.

A Democratic Transfer of Power

Violeta Barrios de Chamorro sought to lead the country to peace and prosperity, and to safeguard human rights and property, but 11 years of war had left its mark. Corruption was widespread, and the business community became impatient with the slow pace of change. Former Managua mayor Arnoldo Alemán won the 1996 presidential election. More than 76 percent of Nicaragua's 2.4 million eligible voters participated. The next highest vote getter was Daniel Ortega, the former president and Sandinista leader. The first transfer of power in recent Nicaraguan history from one democratically elected president to another took place on January 10, 1997, when the Alemán government was inaugurated.

The presidents of 34 nations in the western hemisphere met in Quebec, Canada, during April 2001 to discuss the creation of a free trade zone. Arnoldo Alemán, president of Nicaragua from 1997 to 2001, is the second person from the right. With him are the heads of other Latin American countries, including (left to right) Said Musa of Belize, Hipolito Mejia of the Dominican Republic, Alfonso Portillo of Guatemala, Miguel Angel Rodriguez of Costa Rica, Francisco Flores Perez of El Salvador, Mireyra Moscoso of Panama, and Carlos Flores of Honduras.

Nicaragua is still recovering slowly. In 1998, Hurricane Mitch devastated the country, killing more than 9,000 people, leaving two million people homeless, and causing $10 billion in damages. Many Nicaraguans fled to the United States under an immigration *amnesty* program extended from the Sandinista era.

A second barrier to economic recovery is that thousands of lawsuits over property clog the Nicaraguan courts. Often, a piece of property is

Two former leaders of Nicaragua: Sandinista leader Daniel Ortega and newspaper publisher Violeta Barrios de Chamorro. Since the Sandinista government fell in the late 1980s, Ortega has run for president three times. He lost the 2001 election despite a "path of love" campaign that stressed harmony.

caught in a three-way battle between those who owned it before the Sandinistas came to power, joint public owners created by the Sandinistas, and former Contra rebels who claim they were promised land for joining the anti-Sandinista forces.

On November 6, 2000, the Sandinista Party candidate won the mayoral election in Managua, Nicaragua's capital and largest city. Some observers believed this was a sign that Nicaraguans were disillusioned with their current government.

However, exactly a year later, during a national presidential election, former Sandinista president Daniel Ortega lost his bid to regain the land's highest office. An enormous turnout of voters, some of who had waited five hours to vote, elected conservative businessman Enrique Bolanos, whose property had been taken by the Sandinistas in the early 1980s. In a speech conceding defeat, Ortega said, "We accept the mandate of the people."

(Opposite) A Nicaraguan woman picks cotton. (Right) Cedar and mahogany logs harvested from Nicaragua's rain forest are loaded onto a truck in the village of Alamikamba. Although the country's economy is improving, Nicaragua remains the second-poorest nation in the western hemisphere.

3 Step-by-Step Improvements in the Economy

SINCE 1991, NICARAGUA has reduced *inflation* from 10,000 percent to 12 percent and attracted foreign investment in its economy. Its traditional exports—coffee, meat, and sugar—continue to be strong. In addition, new items, such as clothing, bananas, gold, and seafood, and new agricultural products, such as sesame and melons, have added to Nicaragua's list of goods sold to other countries. However, Nicaragua remains one of the poorest nations in the western hemisphere, with huge debts owed to other countries. Nations such as the United States that control *foreign aid* through the International Monetary Fund (IMF) have insisted that Nicaragua take more steps to reduce poverty, maintain fair government, and guarantee respect for human rights.

An Economy in Recovery

In the last quarter of the 20th century, Nicaragua's economy suffered. An earthquake in 1972 destroyed property. In 1979, the takeover by Sandinista rebels ushered in an 11-year economic decline. Then in 1998, destruction by Hurricane Mitch caused more financial setbacks. On the other hand, since the election of Violeta Chamorro in 1990 and a return to democracy, Nicaragua has experienced rapid growth that is continuing into the 21st century.

About two-fifths of Nicaragua's workers are engaged in agriculture, forestry, and fishing, which produce about one-fourth of the total national income. In the mid-1990s Nicaragua's main export products were coffee, seafood, beef, and sugar. Crops grown by farmers for their own use included corn, beans, rice, sorghum, plantains, and cassava. Other homegrown fruits and vegetables, too many to name, are also raised by Nicaraguans for their own tables. Cattle are a major a source of hides, meat, and

Working in the shadow of Nicaragua's San Cristobal volcano, a farmer uses a machete to cultivate his field.

dairy products in the west and of meat in the east. Other livestock include goats, hogs, horses, and sheep.

Forestry and the production of lumber were expanding rapidly until the fighting between Sandinistas and Contras destroyed the sawmills in the 1980s. With one-third of the country covered by forest, however, it is possible that this activity will revive.

Shrimping is the most important fishing activity in Nicaragua, with most of the catch from the Pacific and Caribbean coasts being sold for export. Lobsters also are exported, but in smaller amounts. Like Nicaragua's forests, the country's fisheries have not become as commercial as they could be, mainly because of lack of investment. Most fishing takes place by families feeding themselves.

In the last 10 years, tourism has poured much-needed money into the Nicaraguan economy. More than 50,000 visitors from the United States visit Nicaragua each year—business people, tourists, and returning relatives. An estimated 5,300 U.S. citizens live permanently in the country. Nicaragua's ecological attractions—beaches, volcanoes, and wildlife—hold the potential to draw many more tourists in the future.

Industry Needing Investment

So far, Nicaragua's industry has been based on producing consumer products—goods to be purchased in stores. But to manufacture them, local businesses must rely heavily on raw material imports. Since the late 1990s, the government has supported creating a greater variety of products using *domestic* raw materials found in Nicaragua. Some of these new products made inside Nicaragua's borders include refined petroleum, matches, footwear, soap and vegetable oils, cement, alcoholic beverages, and textiles.

Of all the country's minerals, only gold has been mined intensively. Mineral reserves in Nicaragua, of which there are many, have not been mined very much because of lack of investment.

Trade on the Upswing

Trade between Nicaragua and other countries is growing. During the Sandinista period in the 1980s, Nicaragua tried not to depend on the United States as a trading partner. When the United States declared a trade embargo on Nicaragua in 1985 due to political conflicts between the two nations, other Western countries purchased Nicaraguan imports instead.

After 1990, trade with the United States resumed. However, from the 1970s through the mid-1990s, the value of Nicaragua's imports—petroleum, some minerals, and industrial product—was greater than the sale of its exports. The result is that Nicaragua's debt burden to other countries continues to act like a brake on its economy, making it hard for local industries to borrow money for investment.

A Limited Transportation System

Most of Nicaragua's transportation system is limited to the Pacific lowlands—the west coast, in other words, where the major cities are located. There is a network of highways, but during the rainy season, roads sometimes wash out. Nicaragua's highway system includes a 255-mile (410 km) section of the Pan-American Highway, which runs through the west from

Quick Facts: The Economy of Nicaragua

Per capita income (2001): $2,650

Natural resources: farmland, livestock, fisheries, gold, timber.

Industry (24 percent of GDP*): Processed food, beverages, textiles, petroleum, and metal products.

Agriculture (32 percent of GDP): Corn, coffee, sugar, meat, rice, beans, bananas.

Services (44 percent of GDP): Commerce, construction, government, banking, transportation, and energy.

Foreign trade (2001): Exports $704 million: coffee, seafood, beef, sugar, industrial goods, gold, bananas, sesame; Imports $1.45 billion: petroleum, agricultural supplies, manufactured goods.

Unemployment rate: 10.5 percent.

Economic growth rate: 5 percent.

Currency exchange rate (2003): 13.5 cordobas = U.S. $1.

* GDP or gross domestic product—the total value of goods and services produced in a year

Honduras to Costa Rica. Another major road runs from the Pan-American Highway, 24 miles from Managua eastward, to Port Esperanza at Rama. A third connects Managua with Puerto Cabezas on the Caribbean.

Railways in Nicaragua total just a few hundred miles. The main line runs from Granada, northwest to Corinto, on the Pacific Ocean. A branch line leads north from León to the coffee area of Carazo.

Ocean ports provide Nicaragua with important trading links to other countries. The chief ocean ports of Corinto, which handles most foreign trade, Puerto Sandino, and San Juan del Sur serve the Pacific coastal area. The ports on the Caribbean side include Puerto Cabezas and Bluefields. The short rivers in the west can be navigated by small craft. In the east, the Coco River is navigable at its lower end for medium-sized vessels.

Demonstrators protest outside the headquarters of the World Bank and International Monetary Fund (IMF) in April 2001. The protesters want the IMF to forgive debts run up by developing nations such as Nicaragua.

Nicaragua has two major airports. The main international airport, seven miles from Managua, has service to North America and Latin America. Another large commercial airport is located at Puerto Cabezas. Other airports have scheduled domestic flights. International air service is offered by one private Nicaraguan firm, Nica, and several U.S. and other foreign airlines.

The Outlook: Promising

Nicaragua has returned to relying heavily on the United States as a trading partner. The United States purchases close to 40 percent of Nicaragua's exports, while Nicaragua receives almost the same amount of its imports from the United States.

Twenty-five wholly or partly owned U.S. companies operate in

Nicaragua. The largest operate in the energy, communications, manufacturing, fisheries, and shrimp farming sectors. Nicaragua hopes to attract more foreign investments in those activities, as well as in tourism, mining, franchising, and the sale of imported consumer, manufacturing, and agricultural goods inside its own borders.

Still, in order to attract continued investment, Nicaragua must comply with an International Monetary Fund (IMF) program to reduce poverty, maintain fair government, and guarantee respect for human rights. Half of Nicaragua's population is below the poverty line. Millions of people rely on the estimated $600 million a year arriving from relatives living abroad. In addition, thousands of cases involving property taken away by the Sandinista government need to be resolved.

After many years of decline, Nicaragua's economy seems on the verge of rapid growth. In the year 2000 it expanded by a very healthy 5 percent. By 2005, Nicaragua and 33 other countries in the western hemisphere hope to create the Free Trade Area of the Americas, which would do away with many trade barriers.

In the future, Nicaragua's location in Central America could become one of its greatest assets. Several Western nations have expressed interest in building a second interoceanic canal, in addition to the Panama Canal, through Nicaragua.

(Opposite) A young Nicaraguan family peers over the doorway of their home in Jinotega. (Right) A farmer prepares to plant coffee beans in Esteli. Nicaragua is one of the least densely populated countries in Central America, although its population is currently growing faster than the population of any other country in the region.

4 A People With Divided Views of Their Country

MOST NICARAGUANS ARE persons of mixed European and Amerindian ancestry. About one-fifth of the population are blacks or whites, who are about equal in number. Less than five percent of the population are Amerindians. More than 80 percent of Nicaraguans are Catholic, with Protestant Christians making up most of the rest. However, the number of Protestant groups in Nicaragua is growing.

The official and most widely spoken language in Nicaragua is Spanish, except in the Caribbean lowlands, where a mix of English, Spanish, and native Indian is spoken.

More than language, however, separates the East and West coasts. "In many ways," says one source about Nicaragua, "[the East] is a completely

35

different country from the Spanish-speaking nation to the west."

Historically, the settlement of Nicaragua has been uneven across the country. In *pre-Columbian* times, the Pacific lowlands, with its fertile soils and relatively mild climate, supported a large, dense population. The forested central highlands held smaller numbers of people. And the hot, muggy Caribbean lowlands were only sparsely populated.

After Spanish settlers arrived in the early 1500s, Nicaragua's basic settlement pattern remained unchanged for 500 years. More than 60 percent of Nicaraguans live within the narrow strip of the Pacific lowlands. About half as many live in the central highlands. And the Caribbean lowlands, covering more than half of the national territory, holds less than 10 percent of the population.

Most Nicaraguans identify themselves as *mestizos*—people of mixed European and Amerindian descent who share a national Hispanic culture. Until the 19th century, there was still a large Amerindian minority in Nicaragua. Gradually, however, most Amerindians have been *assimilated* into the Hispanic mainstream culture. Today, the country's racial composition is roughly as follows: *mestizo*, 70 percent; European, 12 percent; Amerindian, 7 percent; and Creoles or people of predominately African ancestry, 11 percent.

Nicaragua has been spared the bitter conflict between whites, *mestizos*, and Amerindians that has torn apart other Latin American countries. However, differences in culture, language, and appearance create friction between *mestizos* of the central highlands and Pacific lowlands and non-*mestizo* minorities of the east or Caribbean lowlands.

Two Miskito children eat sugar cane in their home in Tasbapauni, a tiny village on the banks of the Prinzapolka River in Nicaragua's Caribbean region. The Miskito are one of three Amerindian tribes native to the region; the others are the Sumo and Rama.

West/East Friction

The west, where the major urban centers are, is populated by Spanish-speaking whites and *mestizos*, both of whom regard themselves as Nicaraguans and participate in its national life of politics, the arts, athletics, and so on. In addition to speaking Spanish, many professional people on the west coast—those in business, government, education, and science—also speak English.

Almost no pockets of separate Amerindian culture remain in the western half of the country. Indian languages on the west coast have disappeared, even though their influence remains in place-names and many nouns in Nicaraguan Spanish. Nicaraguans sometimes make mention of the

"Indian" *barrios* of Monimbó Amerindians in Masaya, of Subtiava Amerindians in León, and to almost-mainstream Matagalpan Amerindians in the central highlands. However, the ways these groups live make them almost identical with *mestizos*.

In the eastern half of Nicaragua, far away from the decision-making centers of power on the other side of the mountains, Amerindians and Creoles prefer to remain apart in language, customs, and lifestyles.

The eastern side of Nicaragua is more diverse than the western side. Even though Spanish-speaking *mestizos* are the largest single group on the east coast, too, the population of that region also includes Miskito, Sumo, and Rama Indians, as well as Black Caribs—also known as Garifuna, the descendants of African slaves and Carib Indians—and Creoles, or English-speaking

Whether living in the eastern or western regions or Nicaragua, most people have one thing in common—grinding poverty. This young boy is scavenging in a Managua garbage dump. The average person makes the equivalent of about $2,700 a year—almost one-tenth of the average American's annual income.

Quick Facts: The People of Nicaragua

Population: 4,812,569

Ethnic groups: 70 percent *mestizo* (mixed Amerindian and white); 12 percent white; 11 percent black; 7 percent Amerindian.

Age structure:
0–14 years: 40 percent
15–64 years: 57 percent
65 years and over: 3 percent

Population growth rate: 3.4 percent

Birth rate: 28.26 births/1,000 population

Infant mortality rate: 34.79 deaths/1,000 live births

Death rate: 4.9 deaths/1,000 population

Life expectancy at birth:
total population: 68.74 years
male: 66.81 years
female: 70.77 years

Total fertility rate: 3.27 children born per woman.

Religions: 83 percent Roman Catholic; 14 percent Protestant, 3 percent other.

Languages: Spanish (official); English and native languages spoken on Atlantic coast.

Literacy: 65.7 percent (1998 est.)

*All figures 2002 estimates, unless otherwise noted.

blacks. The Amerindians of the eastern half of the country remain ethnically separate and still use tribal customs and languages. Many live in small communities in the rainforest on the eastern slopes of the Central highlands.

In the mid-1980s, the Sandinista government divided the eastern side of Nicaragua into two separate regions and granted the people limited self-rule. Under the 1987 constitution and the Atlantic Coast Autonomy Law enacted the same year, Miskito, Sumo, Rama, and Creole-English were given equal rank in public life with Spanish. Constitutional reform in 1995 further guaranteed that the region's unique cultures would be respected and gave the inhabitants a voice in how the area's natural resources would be used.

These measures gave peoples on the east coast greater self-determination. But in another way, they were also an official way of saying that the interests of the non-*mestizo* population are different from most of the rest of Nicaragua.

Religion and Education

There is no official religion in Nicaragua, but most people practice Roman Catholicism. In the 1980s, Protestantism won over tens of thousands of *converts*, owing to missionary work and preaching by Christian fundamentalists. Very small Jewish communities also can be found in Nicaragua's larger cities.

The literacy rate in Nicaragua—the percentage of the population older than 15 who can read and write—is high compared to other Central American countries. During the Sandinista era of the 1980s, a massive learn-to-read campaign raised the literacy rate significantly higher.

Schooling in Nicaragua in the primary and secondary grades is free and *compulsory*. However, many children cannot attend because there no local schools, especially in *rural* areas. Also, children are expected to help their families at an early age, even if that means getting a full-time job. Most drop out long before high school. Only about 20 percent of children who start school reach high school. There are universities in Nicaragua, which have been attracting an increasing number of students in recent years.

A Population Boom

Since the 1950s, Nicaragua has had a high birth rate, coupled with rapid urban growth. Both trends are expected to continue for decades.

Despite the loss of nearly 31,000 Nicaraguans killed during the Contra War during the 1980s and the hundreds of thousands who took refuge abroad, Nicaragua's population exploded from 2.5 million to nearly 4 million during the Sandinista rule.

In 1990, an estimated 3.87 million people lived in Nicaragua. The population had tripled in the preceding 25 years and is expected to double again by 2015. In the late 1980s, the population was expanding at a rate of 3.4 percent annually, far above the Central American average of 2.1 percent for the same period.

Children attend classes at the Las Torres elementary school in Managua. Although education is free in Nicaragua, there are few schools, especially in rural areas. Many children drop out before reaching high school.

Continuing high birth rates, together with a decline in the percent of infant deaths over the years, have produced a young population. In 1990, nearly half of the population of Nicaragua was younger than 15 years old. More elderly are seen in Nicaragua, too. Life expectancy at birth lengthened

Did You Know?

- Nicaragua has a republic-type government which consists of executive, legislative, and judicial branches. Its current constitution was adopted on January 9, 1987, and reformed in 1995 and 2000.
- The president and vice president are elected on the same ticket by popular vote for a five-year term; in the October 2001 election, Enrique Bolanos was elected president of Nicaragua.
- There are 93 seats in Nicaragua's National Assembly. Members are elected by proportional representation to serve five-year terms)
- The Supreme Court, or *Corte Suprema*, consists of 16 judges elected for seven-year terms by the National Assembly.
- Major political parties in Nicaragua include the Liberal Alliance (AL), and the Sandinista National Liberation Front (FSLN).
- The capital of Nicaragua is Managua.
- The voting age is 16.

from about 45 years of age in the late 1950s to 62 years of age in the 1991 due to better health care.

An Urban Society

By 1993, Nicaragua was rapidly turning into an urban society. Groups of *shantytowns* growing around the larger cities provide proof of the rapid pace of change. About 60 percent of the population lived in urban areas in 2000.

Although birth rates in the towns and cities are much lower than they are in the countryside, people moving from the countryside to cities and towns has resulted in the faster growth of the urban population. From 1970 to 1990, the urban population in Nicaragua swelled to bursting at an annual rate of 4 percent. This means some cities almost doubled in size in 20 years. By comparison, the rural population grew at only 2.3 percent. Much of the urban growth has happened in the capital city of Managua.

Managua's population was just 7.5 percent of the total national population in 1940; 15 percent by 1960; and 28 percent by 1980. By 2000, Managua's population was estimated at well over 1 million. No other Nicaraguan city is anywhere near that size. The country's second-largest city is León, with a population of roughly 130,000 in 1990. The other important cities, all with populations ranging from 50,000 to 100,000, are Matagalpa, Masaya, and Granada. Somewhat smaller are the principal towns on the Caribbean coast: Bluefields and Puerto Cabezas. However, accurate estimates of populations of Nicaraguan cities have not been available since the 1970s.

The Challenges of Rapid Growth

Nicaragua's explosive population growth and the rapid expansion of its cities and towns are two serious problems facing the country. High birth rates strain the country's inadequate health and education systems. Added to this, an expanding population takes a heavy toll on the environment. Also, cities that are growing require expensive investment in transportation and sanitation.

Despite these problems, Nicaraguan governments—including that of the Sandinistas—have not made population control a national goal. This is chiefly because Nicaraguans are divided over the issue. Although some are concerned about the consequences of rapid growth, others point out that Nicaragua has the lowest number of persons per square mile in Central America. Overpopulation, they argue, is not likely to happen. In addition, the Nicaraguan Roman Catholic Church and other Roman Catholic leaders have repeatedly objected to birth control on religious grounds.

(Opposite) A man offers an iguana for sale on the streets of Managua. Because of the country's overall poverty, some Nicaraguans are willing to sell even endangered animals in order to make a living. (Right) A laboratory worker in the Nicaraguan Archaeology Department cleans a human skull found in the remains of a 17th-century church in Granada.

5 An Identity Still Evolving

WITH A POPULATION of four million people and a history created from the overlap between an Amerindian and European past, Nicaragua offers an uneven mix of culture and tradition. The majority of Nicaraguans, including *mestizos*, whites and blacks, share a Hispanic culture. On the Caribbean coast, non-Spanish speaking and non-Catholic people prefer a blend of English and native culture. The Sandinista revolution of 1979 and the civil war of the 1980s shook the foundation of the entire country, however, leaving many Nicaraguans wondering what their national identity will be in the future.

The majority of Nicaraguans—those who live on the Pacific coast— have developed their culture from a mixture of the native Indians and the

45

Spanish settlers of the 16th century. Consequently, many of the cities retain a strong Spanish influence, and Catholicism is the most widely practiced religion.

The Caribbean coast, on the other hand, was more influenced by the English who controlled that region until the 19th century. Blacks and native peoples—Miskito, Rama, and Sumu—preferred to deal with the British rather than the Spanish and adapted some of their ways. For example, in the southeastern town of Bluefields, where many blacks live who are descended from slaves, the annual celebration of *Mayo Ya* combines English Maypole dancing with Caribbean folklore and African music and dance. Bluefields is also home to reggae music. Added to this, Protestant religions are more common here than on the Pacific coast, although Catholicism is still the dominant religion. Outside of this interesting mix of culture and tradition, some Amerindians living in this region prefer to remain largely non-Western in their ways altogether.

The Catholic Heritage

The majority of Nicaraguans are Catholic, and most communities observe a religious calendar dotted with festive parades honoring the local patron saint. Each city in Nicaragua has its own patron saint, and some saints are shared between towns. Devout people offer gifts to saints in exchange for blessings, such as healing, a good crop, or children. Part of the tradition of honoring a saint is holding a fiesta, too.

Fiestas are holidays of fun and excitement in villages, towns, and cities. A statue of the saint being honored is carried through the streets, signaling the start of traditional dances, plays, or rituals. Following the saint's images, people offer flower arrangements, and they pay their "promises" with little gold and silver objects and fruit bunches. As night falls, exploding firecrackers and fireworks add to the pleasure of entertainment by roving musicians, performing clowns, and speeches by local leaders.

Literature: a National Passion

Literature is one of Nicaragua's most popular arts. Works by Rubén Darío (1867–1916), known as the "prince of Spanish-American poetry," and recent works by Nicaraguan poets, fiction writers, and essayists can be found in most bookshops. Although Darío spent much time outside Nicaragua, he wrote often about the conflicting beauties of his homeland.

Even in literature, however, issues of race, class, and national identity divide Nicaraguans. To some, the works of Darío are examples of literature aimed at the professional class of better-educated people. The revolutionary period from the late 1970s through 1990 produced another kind of artistic expression. Unlike the Somoza regime, which had valued traditional 19th-century Western culture, the Sandinistas supported what they termed "democratizing, national, anti-*imperialist*" art forms, both professional and amateur.

The Sandinistas appointed poet and priest Ernesto Cardenal head of a Ministry of Culture. Cardenal had retreated for a time to the island of Solentiname in Lake Nicaragua to write poetry and encourage a settlement of artists, writers, and craftspeople. The Sandinistas also created an Association of Cultural Workers under the leadership of poet Rosario

Murillo. Both organizations built museums, sponsored professional artists, and created popular workshops to nurture the talents of citizens. But when the economy collapsed in the late 1980s, the Ministry of Culture was closed.

Today, Nicaragua's museums and libraries are small and poorly maintained. The National Library and the National Museum in Managua, as well as the Rubén Darío museum in Ciudad Darío, were created before the revolution and are now in poor condition. The Museum of the Revolution and the Museum of the Literacy Crusade in Managua, the Sandino Museum in Niquinohomo, and others—all created by the Sandinistas—were abandoned after 1990.

On the other hand, folk traditions in Nicaragua continue to be strong and expressed in arts and crafts, popular religious ceremonies, and country songs (*corridos*). Many Nicaraguan folktales involve magic cures and evil spells. Some of the eeriest come from the people of Ometepe, an island in Lake Nicaragua with two volcanoes. These teach respect for nature and show how humans sometimes mistreat each other.

Architecture from Long Ago

Earthquakes and war have destroyed much of Nicaragua's colonial architecture, though some still remains. Many of Nicaragua's landmark buildings are in Granada and León, the two cities that have long served as the country's military, cultural, and religious centers.

Fine examples of colonial architecture in Granada begin with La Merced Church, the construction of which began in 1543. The main Cathedral of Granada makes up one side of the central plaza, as cathedrals do in all Spanish colonial cities. Xalteva Church, and the walls that surround its neighborhood, date to the early 17th century.

The original city of León, at the foot of the Momotombo volcano, was destroyed by an earthquake in 1609, but the ruins have been *excavated*. In the resettled city of León, the Metropolitan Cathedral represents massive religious architecture from the mid-18th century and is the largest cathedral in Central America. This cathedral not only houses artistic masterpieces, it is also the final resting place of the country's most prestigious figures, including the poet Rubén Darío, who is buried at the foot of a statue of St. Paul and guarded by a sorrowful lion.

Food, Drink, and Music

The Nicaraguan food, like many dishes in Central American, is based on corn. Corn has a deep cultural mean-

Children line up for a festive meal.

In a parade in Managua, children wear masks to represent Spanish visitors to Nicaragua. The parade is part of the country's October 12 celebration of Columbus Day, marking the date of the explorer's arrival in the New World.

ing. Quetzalcoatl, a mythical hero who guided the Amerindians, put a grain of corn on the lips of the first man and woman, enabling them to think and work. Today, corn is the main ingredient used in many dishes, drinks, desserts, and other refreshments. Cassava (yucca), beans, and chili peppers are also widely used as ingredients in different Nicaraguan dishes.

A typical meal in Nicaragua consists of eggs or meat, beans and rice, salad (cabbage and tomatoes), tortillas, and fruit in season. Food is usually scooped

Did You Know?

Nicaragua's flag consists of three equal horizontal bands of blue (top), white, and blue with the national coat of arms centered in the white band. The coat of arms features a triangle encircled by the words *Republica De Nicaragua* on the top and *America Central* on the bottom.

up in tortillas instead of using knives and forks. Most common of all Nicaraguan foods is *gallo pinto*, a blend of rice and beans. Other traditional dishes include *bajo* (a mix of beef, green and ripe plantains, and cassava) and *vigorón* (cassava served with fried pork skins and coleslaw). Street vendors sell drinks such as *tiste*, made from cacao and corn, and *posol con leche*, a corn-and-milk drink. Roasted corn on the cob is also sold on the streets. Restaurants, particularly in Managua, serve a variety of foods, including Spanish, Italian, French, Latin American, and Chinese.

> ## Did You Know?
>
> These are the official holidays in Nicaragua. Other occasions are celebrated with parties and carnivals or family get-togethers. In addition, many towns hold a *festejo*, or festival, to honor its patron saint.
>
> - January 1—New Year's Day
> - May 1—Labor Day
> - May 30—Mothers' Day
> - July 19—National Liberation Day
> - August 1—Fiesta Day
> - September 14—San Jacinto Fight Day
> - September 15—Independence Day
> - November 2—All Souls Day
> - December 8—Feast of the Immaculate Conception
> - December 25—Christmas Day

The marimba is the national instrument. It is constructed from hardwood plates, placed over bamboo or metal tubes of different lengths. The tubes are played using two soft hammers, like a xylophone. The marimba blends well with guitars and percussion instruments.

During festival times, people look forward to seeing traditional dances and skits performed to music. The most popular are "Los Caballeros Elegantes del Toro Huaco" (The Elegant Knights of the Huaco Bull), "La Burla del Güegüense" (The Güegüense Trick), and "El Drama Épico del Gigante" (The Amazing Story of the Giants).

Recipes

Fresco de Piña y Arroz (Pineapple and Rice Drink)

(Makes 6 to 8 cups)
16-oz. can of sliced pineapple
1/2 cup rice
strainer
sugar

Directions:
1. Place drained pineapple slices in a pot. Add enough water to cover by about two inches.
2. Bring to a boil for about 10 minutes, and then add about 1/2 cup of uncooked white rice. Keep boiling until the rice splits or puffs.
3. Let cool. Strain out the liquid.
4. Add about twice as much water as you got from the pot. Add sugar to taste. Drink very cold.

Picos

(Serves about 12)
Refrigerated biscuit dough
Brown sugar
Quajada—a soft cheese from Nicaragua (you can use farmer's cheese instead)

Directions:
1. Roll the bread dough thin, and cut into large triangles.
2. Place about half a teaspoon of brown sugar and a small piece of cheese in the center of the triangle. Fold over the other corners of the triangle and overlap them in the center.
3. Bake until the bread is browned.

Tres Leches (Three Milks)—a cake

(Makes one 12" x 8" cake)
5 eggs
1 cup white sugar
1 cup self-rising flour
1 teaspoon vanilla extract
1 small can sweetened condensed milk
1 small can evaporated milk
1/2 cup milk
1 tablespoon vanilla extract
3 egg whites
1 cup white sugar
1 tablespoon vanilla extract

Directions:
1. Grease and flour an 8 x 12 inch pan. Preheat the oven to 350° F.
2. Separate the 5 eggs, and beat the egg whites in a large mixing bowl. Add the cup of sugar slowly to the egg whites, beating constantly. Add the yolks one by one, beating well after each addition. Stir in the teaspoon of vanilla.
3. Sift the flour, and stir it into the egg mixture.
4. Pour the batter into the prepared pan. Bake the cake for 20 minutes or until done. Cool.
5. Blend the sweetened condensed milk, evaporated milk, milk, and a tablespoon of vanilla. Pour over the cooled cake. (The cake is meant to be a little soggy. Keep it refrigerated.)
To make meringue frosting: Beat 3 egg whites to soft peaks. Gradually add 1 cup sugar, and beat until stiff peaks form. Stir in 1 teaspoon vanilla. Frost the cake.

Chocolate Bananas

(Makes 16)
8 firm bananas (not too ripe)
2 small cans of chocolate syrup
16 Popsicle sticks
A knife
Wax paper

Directions:
1. Peel bananas and cut in half.
2. Stick a Popsicle stick into each banana, making sure it goes in straight.
3. Coat the bananas with chocolate syrup by dipping them into a tall glass filed with the syrup.
4. Place the bananas on wax paper over a plate or cookie sheet, and put the bananas into a freezer until frozen.

Gallo Pinto (Speckled Rooster)

(This dish gets its name from the appearance of the mixture. It does not actually contain rooster or any other type of meat. Serves 12)
2 tablespoons of oil
1/2 cup chopped onions
1 teaspoon red chili powder
8 12-oz. cans of pinto beans
2 cups cooked white rice

Directions:
1. Heat oil in a large skillet (don't let it smoke).
2. Add chili powder and onions. Fry until the onions are golden.
3. Mix equal portions of cooked red beans and cooked white rice, and stir-fry in oil until tender. The rice should be a little brown.

Glossary

Amerindians—native peoples of the Americas.

Amnesty—the act of an authority (as a government) by which pardon is granted to a large group of individuals.

Assassinate—to murder by sudden or secret attack.

Assimilate—to integrate somebody into a larger group, so that differences are minimized or eliminated; cultural blending.

Barrio—a ghetto, or ethnic communities.

Cay—a low island or reef of sand or coral.

Civil rights—rights of personal liberty.

Compulsory—something that is required by law; mandatory.

Convert—someone who has changed religious beliefs.

Destabilize—to make something, particularly a government or economy, unstable.

Domestic—relating to the internal affairs of a nation or country.

Excavate—to dig out and remove.

Foreign aid—financial assistance given by one country to another.

Guerrilla—an irregular armed force.

Imperialist—one country extending power over another.

Indigenous—native.

Infertile—inadequate for growing.

Inflation—when the purchasing power of money drops.

Leftists—those who favor Communist or Socialist ideas.

Martial—relating to an army or to military life.

Pre-Columbian—a term referring to the period of American history before the arrival of Christopher Columbus at the end of the 15th century.

Regime—a government, especially one that is considered to be oppressive.

Resin—a natural substance formed by plant secretions and used chiefly in varnishes, printing inks, plastics, and in medicine.

Rural—in the countryside.

Shantytowns—villages made of shacks.

Tectonic—having to do with the plates of the earth's crust, or surface.

Terrain—shape of the landscape.

Trade embargo—a refusal to trade goods and services.

Trade wind—a wind blowing almost constantly in one direction.

Project and Report Ideas

Create a map of Nicaragua's west

Make a layered map by using several transparency sheets. On one, draw the natural features of Nicaragua; on a second, place the major cities and towns; on a third, show the highways, rail lines, and airports. Place each one on top of the other on a transparency projector to show classmates how Nicaragua is "tilted toward the west" in terms of its population and development.

Create a "climate map" of Nicaragua

Using transparencies, show the three lands of Nicaragua—the hot land, the mild land, and the cold land.

Create a map of Nicaragua's food resources

Using this book, an encyclopedia, and the Internet as resources, find out the areas where important fruits, trees, and vegetables of Nicaragua are grown. Draw a map of the country, pointing out which foods are grown in which regions. You could also show where fishing takes place.

Flashcards

Using the glossary in this book, create flashcards. Put the term on one side and the definition on the other. Practice with the cards in pairs. Then, choose two teams of three. Select a referee to say the term out loud, and then call on someone to give the definition. The referee's decision is final. Award points for each correct answer. You can also read the definition, and ask for the correct term instead!

Presentations

- Memorize and recite two poems by Rubén Darío (you can find translations on the Internet).
- Find three pieces of marimba music, and play them for the class. Explain each title. (Your local reference librarian can help you.)

- There are letters on the Internet written by American students studying abroad in Nicaragua. Find one and read it aloud to the class. Does it give you any insights into the country?

Reports

Write one-page, five-paragraph reports answering any of the following questions. Begin with a paragraph of introduction, then three paragraphs each developing one main idea, followed by a conclusion that summarizes your topic:

- Why are there sharks in Lake Nicaragua.
- Who were the Caribbean pirates and how did they live?
- What was the Iran-Contra Affair? What was the result?
- Who built the Pan-American Highway? Where does it go?
- What is the International Monetary Fund? Where does it get its money? What does it do?
- Draw pictures and provide one-paragraph descriptions of any five animals of Nicaragua mentioned in Chapter One, "A Land Rich in Natural Resources."

Write one-page biographies of any one of these people:

Francisco Hernández de Córdoba	Cornelius Vanderbilt	William Walker
General Augusto Sandino	Anastasio Somoza Debayle	Daniel Ortega
Oscar Arias Sánchez	Rubén Darío	

Chronology

1509	Spanish settlers arrive in Panama; by 1524, the Spanish have moved into the rest of Central America.
1821	The confederation of Central American provinces proclaims its independence from Spain.
1855	American mercenary William Walker is hired by a Nicaraguan political party to topple the president; he takes control of the government and sets himself up as president; he is ousted the next year.
1909	Dictator Jose Santos Zelaya is overthrown in Nicaragua; chaos and instability follow, leading to U.S. financial and military intervention.
1927	Potential peace accord among fighting factions in Nicaragua provides basis for U.S. occupation and subsequent elections; General Augusto C. Sandino refuses to accept peace accord and leads a guerrilla force against the U.S. Marines.
1931	An earthquake destroys most of the capital city of Managua.
1933	General Anastasio Somoza Garcia is named director of the new National Guard in Nicaragua; the U.S. Marines withdraw.
1934	Sandino is murdered by members of the Nicaraguan National Guard; Guard chief Anastasio Somoza Garcia dominates the country until 1956.
1956	Anastasio Somoza is assassinated; his sons, Luis and Anastasio Jr., retain control of Nicaragua.
1961	The Sandinista National Liberation Front (FSLN) is founded in Nicaragua.
1967	Anastasio Somoza Debayle is "elected" president of Nicaragua.
1972	An earthquake devastates Managua; Somoza's mishandling of crisis and of international relief funds increases anger toward the regime.

Chronology

1972	The assassination of crusading journalist Pedro Joaquín Chamorro by a Somoza henchman increases opposition to the Somoza dictatorship.
1979	Somoza is overthrown, and a new governing coalition dominated by the Sandinistas assumes power.
1981	The U.S. ends aid to Nicaragua after finding evidence that Nicaragua, Cuba, and the Soviet Union are supplying arms to rebels in El Salvador.
1984	Daniel Ortega, leader of the FSLN, is "elected" president of Nicaragua.
1985	The U.S. suspends talks and trade with Nicaragua.
1986	The U.S. government announces the Reagan administration has been providing military aid to the Contras; the supplies were purchased using funds diverted from the sale of U.S. arms to Iran; the covert operation became known as the Iran-Contra Affair.
1987	Peace talks between the Sandinistas and the Contras break down; Ortega confirms rumors that the Soviets plan to supply Nicaragua with more military aid.
1988	The Sandinistas and Contras begin a cease-fire and are parties to a peace plan developed by Oscar Arias Sánchez of Costa Rica.
1990	Violeta Barrios de Chamorro of the UNO party (National Opposition Union) defeats the FSLN's Daniel Ortega in internationally observed presidential elections; Sandinistas and Contras sign a permanent cease-fire.
1997	Arnoldo Alemán is inaugurated as president, thus completing the first democratic and peaceful transfer of the presidency in Nicaragua's history.
2001	Sandinista candidate Daniel Ortega is defeated in fall presidential election.
2002	Enrique Bolanos takes office as president of Nicaragua.

Further Reading/Internet Resources

Cerar, K. Melissa. *Teenage Refugees from Nicaragua Speak Out.* New York: Rosen Publishing Group, 1997.

Cummins, Ronnie. *Nicaragua.* Milwaukee: G. Stevens Children's Books, 1990.

Glassman, Paul. *Nicaragua Guide.* Champlain: Travel Line Press, 1995.

Griffiths, John. *Nicaragua.* Philadelphia: Chelsea House Publishers, 1998.

Haverstock, Nathan A. *Nicaragua in Pictures.* Minneapolis: Lerner Publications, 1993.

Henderson, James D. *A Reference Guide to Latin American History.* Armonk, N.Y.: M. E. Sharpe, 2000.

Marriot, Edward. *Savage Shore: Life and Death with Nicaragua's Last Shark Hunters.* New York: Owl Books, 2001.

Plunkett, Hazel. *Nicaragua.* New York: Interlink Publishing Group, 1999.

Rohmer, Harriet, Octavia Chow, and Morris Vidaure. *The Invisible Hunters: A Legend of the Miskito Indians of Nicaragua.* San Francisco: Children's Book Press, 1987.

Woodward, Ralph Lee Jr. *Central America: A Nation Divided*, 3rd ed. New York: Oxford University Press, 1999.

Travel information

http://www.nicaragua-online.com/
http://www.lonelyplanet.com/destinations/central_america/nicaragua/

History and Geography

http://lanic.utexas.edu/
http://www.britannica.com/eb/article?eu=118733&tocid=214487#214487.toc
http://www.guideofnicaragua.com.ni/Junio/BasicFacts/BasicFacts.html

Economic and Political Information

http://www.britannica.com/eb/article?eu=118730&tocid=40978#40978.toc
http://www.countrywatch.com/files/126/cw_country.asp?vCOUNTRY=126
http://www.state.gov/www/background_notes/nicar_0009_bgn.html

**American Chamber of Commerce
in Nicaragua**
Apartado Postal 202
Managua, Nicaragua
(505) 267-3099

Caribbean/Latin American Action
1818 N Street NW, Suite 310
Washington, D.C. 20036
(202) 466-7464

Embassy of Nicaragua
1627 New Hampshire Avenue NW
Washington, D.C. 20009
(202) 939-6570

**Permanent Representative of
Nicaragua to the United Nations**
820 Second Avenue, 8th Floor
New York, N.Y. 10017 USA
(212) 490-7997

U.S. Department of Commerce
International Trade Administration
Trade Information Center
14th and Constitution NW
Washington, D.C. 20230
1-800-USA-TRADE

Index

Contributors

Senior Consulting Editor **James D. Henderson** is professor of international studies at Coastal Carolina University. He is the author of *Conservative Thought in Twentieth Century Latin America: The Ideals of Laureano Gómez* (1988; Spanish edition *Las ideas de Laureano Gómez* published in 1985); *When Colombia Bled: A History of the Violence in Tolima* (1985; Spanish edition *Cuando Colombia se desangró, una historia de la Violencia en metrópoli y provincia*, 1984); and co-author of *A Reference Guide to Latin American History* (2000) and *Ten Notable Women of Latin America* (1978).

   Mr. Henderson earned a bachelors degree in history from Centenary College of Louisiana, and a masters degree in history from the University of Arizona. He then spent three years in the Peace Corps, serving in Colombia, before earning his doctorate in Latin American history in 1972 at Texas Christian University.

Charles J. Shields, the author of all eight books in the DISCOVERING CENTRAL AMERICA series, lives in Homewood, a suburb of Chicago, with his wife Guadalupe, an elementary-school principal. He has a degree in history from the University of Illinois in Urbana-Champaign, and was chairman of the English department and the guidance department at Homewood-Flossmoor High School in Flossmoor, Illinois.